Writing the Killer Mystery

Volume Five

Getting It Right, Getting Paid

The Keys to Making
Your Mystery Novel a Winner

by

Ron D. Voigts

Ron D. Voigts

Writing the Killer Mystery, Getting It Right, Getting Paid

Copyright © 2019 by Ron D. Voigts

All material and information in this book are considered factual and accurate to the author's and publisher's knowledge.

Paperback edition: January 2019 Night Wings Publishing

ISBN: 978-1795288798

Ron D. Voigts

Dedication

To my wife, Lois,

who has stuck with me and understood me

even when nobody else does

Ron D. Voigts

Books by Ron D. Voigts

Self-Published

Penelope and The Birthday Curse

Penelope and The Ghost's Treasure

Penelope and The Movie Star

Penelope and The Christmas Spirit

Claws of the Griffin

Night Wings Publishing

Strigoi, The Blood Bond

Champagne Book Group

The Witch's Daughter

The Fortune Teller's Secret

Writing the Killer Mystery

Volume One, Great Beginnings

Volume Two, Captivating Characters

Volume Three, Plotting the Murder

Volume Four, Places, Clues and Guilt

Volume Five, Getting It Right, Getting Paid

Ron D. Voigts

TABLE OF CONTENTS

CHAPTER SIX: MARKETING, YOU GOT TO HAVE A PLAN.....41

CHAPTER SEVEN: LAST THOUGHTS 59

Chapter One:
Front End Stuff

First things first, I don't like reading forwards, prologues, and front end matter. Get me to the good stuff. However, I have a philosophy behind this book, the series, in fact. So stop back later if you wish to jump ahead.

I planned a five-volume series on **Writing the Killer Mystery** with some goals.

- Ideally, from beginning to end, these five volumes should give an excellent working knowledge of writing a mystery. Articles appear under broader headings and can be read in series-order to gain better insight into an aspect of mystery writing.

- The series is not just to inform but to inspire. Need help in finding a motive, examine the list in that section. Trying to come up with something on your sleuth's background, a list of ideas is available for your perusal. If you're stumped how to create a supervillain, a list exists for that too. Remember, these suggestions are the beginnings to stimulate your imagination. You are the author of your mystery.

- I have another philosophy. My time to read, write, handle social media, keep up with current events, take time for entertainment, and have a social life pretty much keeps me busy from dawn to bedtime, so finding moments to get absorbed in a book are hard. So, I wrote this volume in bite-size chunks to be read in short sittings. Key points, bullets, numberings, and lists are used where possible to make things easier. Examples happen at the end of many sections if more understanding is needed. The whole point is to get information fast and easy.

- The articles can stand-alone too. If you are struggling to name your sleuth, stop by that section in Volume Two for inspiration. Read the article on guns in Volume Four if you need some background. By the way, I wrote this for writers. If you check out the gun section to learn how to field strip a Glock and reassemble it, you are looking in the wrong place. Articles for nearly every facet of mystery writing can be found in the five volumes.

Following is a brief summary of contents of this fourth volume in **Writing the Killer Mystery**.

- Writing Advice

- Revision

- Self-publishing and traditional publishing

- Marketing

The ultimate goal of Volume Five is to get your mystery ready for publication and marketing. The purpose of Getting It Right, Getting Paid is to make your mystery novel a winner.

Chapter Two:
A Bit of Writing Advice

Point-of-View, Yours, His, Mine

Point-of-view (POV) is the narrator of the story. When done well, most readers are unaware of the POV character in a scene, in a novel. Do it wrong, and it sticks out. In the murder mystery, first-person and third-person POVs occur most often.

First-Person Narrative

The viewpoint of "I" tells the story. She never references herself by her own name. Other characters will reference the "I" narrator her name. First-person story telling allows the reader to identify with the main character. For beginning writers, this POV is the easiest to use. But beware of the tendency to chattiness which leads to sloppy writing.

Often the narration is from the sleuth's point-of-view, sometimes from another's, like the sidekick. Either way, this POV offers an up close, personal experience for the reader.

First-Person, Detective Narrator

Philip Marlowe series by Raymond Chandler

Dave Robicheaux series by James Lee Burke

Lew Archer series by Ross McDonald

Spenser Series by Robert B. Parker

First-Person, Sidekick Narrator

Hercule Poirot by Agatha Christie, Arthur Hastings narrator in some books

Sherlock Holmes series by Sir Arthur Conan Doyle, John Watson narrator

3

Nero Wolfe series by Rex Stout, Archie Goodwin

Third-Person Narrative

Narration comes from the point-of-view of "he" or "she." The narration can identify the POV person by his or her name. Multiple point-of-views tell the tale from different perspectives. Third-person is less intimate.

Third-Person, Detective Narrator

Harry Bosch series by Michael Connelly

Perry Mason series by Erle Stanley Gardner

Jesse Stone series by Robert B. Parker

Point-of-View Considerations

1. Avoid head hopping. A scene should stay consistent in a single POV. Change POV only at a scene change.

2. "Unreliable" narrator. The story is from a first-person POV where the narrator may not be telling the truth. The twist comes at the story's end when the truth becomes known. An excellent example is *The Murder of Roger Ackroyd* by Agatha Christie.

3. The viewpoint limits the POV character to what she thinks, sees, hears, touches, smells, and tastes. Other characters can only be observed and tell their experiences.

4. Make sure the POV character is true to his personality profile and not just reflecting the writer's make-up. This especially becomes a problem when writing in the first-person.

5. When writing in the first-person, avoid excessive use of "I."

6. If the killer or suspects are POV characters, take care not to tip off the reader too soon who-did-it. Narration from the

killers POV may later make the reader feel cheated he didn't know the truth. Best not to use the killer's POV.

7. Typically, the sleuth appears in most of the scenes, so the dominant, most often used, POV will be his or hers.

8. When various POVs occur, set up early in the scene whose POV is narrating.

9. When using multiple POVs in a novel, limit the number, keeping it as minimal as possible.

10. When using more than one POVs and the primary POV (typically the sleuth) appears in a scene, use his or her viewpoint for the scene.

Web of Lies

Lies, lies, lies

They're the threads passing through the mystery, binding it together.

Suspects lie to the sleuth. The killer lies to the sleuth. Suspects and killers lie to each other. Why this taste for untruths? Because secrets abound.

The most obvious secret is the one the killer keeps; he murdered someone. But other lies exist.

Suspects lie to protect themselves or someone else. They hide illicit love affairs and secrets of others. Suspects put themselves into jeopardy to protect others. Who were you with? What did you do? Where were you? The answers can be painful and sometimes dangerous. Even if they killed no one, the truth of the moment may harm themselves.

In the mystery plot, four things happen. The suspect tells his or her story. Snooping by the sleuth will unravel things. A lie becomes clear and casts a specter of guilt on the suspect. Finally, the truth comes out.

The ultimate truth will be the unraveling the killer's lie.

Someone Murdered Ricky

Suspect: Fred

His Story: he and Ethyl, Ricky's wife, are having an affair. To protect Ethyl, he makes up a story of being at the movies, not telling he was with Ethyl at a motel.

Sleuth Snooping: determines that Fred could not have been at the movies because the theater was closed for renovations.

The Lie: Fred's lie and involvement with Ethyl makes him a prime suspect in Ricky's death.

The Truth: the sleuth finds a video from a security camera at the motel, showing Fred and Ethyl were not near the crime scene.

Suspect: Margo

Her Story: she has a doctorate degree from a European school. She came to this country to work with Ricky on bionic research.

Sleuth Snooping: discovers she changed her name and faked the degree.

The Lie: could she have used the fake credentials to get near Ricky and kill him?

The Truth: she has a degree but changed her name to avoid a boyfriend who is stalking her.

Suspect: Kane

His Story: says he did not know the victim.

Sleuth Snooping: learns Kane is Ricky's half-brother, same mother, different father.

Lie: does a family connection mean he's the killer?

Truth: he wanted to make it as a scientist on his own, not because he was the famous researcher's brother.

Suspect: Tina

Story: Says Sol was with her at the time of the murder.

Sleuth Snooping: uncovers Tina was in jail and could not have been with Sol.

The Lie: she lied and Sol's alibi falls apart.

The Truth: Tina owed Sol for supplying her drugs.

Remember, other characters lie too, not just suspects.

And the killer has his own story of what happened, making him appear not guilty. The sleuth's snooping uncovers this lie. The final truth proves the killer did it.

Giving your characters lies and secrets adds depth to the plot and keeps the reader engaged. Creating a web of lies makes a page turner.

Web of Lies Plan
Suspect
His or Her Story
Sleuth Snooping
The Lie
The Truth

Secrets = Lies

Conflict Makes the World Go Round

In a perfect world, nothing bad ever happens. Everyone gets along. Nobody gets hurt. And books don't get written. Why? Because nothing happens to write about.

But we live in the real world. Things don't work well. People disagree. Problems exist. Terrible things happen. One word describes it.

Conflict.

Books get written and conflict keeps the pages turning.

Every scene needs conflict. Every story has it. Two people meet with different ideas. Differing opinions abound. Agendas clash. Even a single character wrestles with personal conflicts.

No conflict means no story.

Conflict becomes the struggle between opposing forces. The sleuth labors to discover who killed the poor victim. The killer strives to avoid detection and arrest. Suspects fight to hide their secrets. Characters struggle with each other outright and on sub-levels of awareness.

A scene needs conflict. No struggle means nothing is happening. Nothing happening is boring. Readers stop turning pages and look for entertainment somewhere else.

Think of your favorite action-packed movie. Stuff is happening. The hero falls out of an airplane with no parachute. Sickos tie up a father and then kill his family while he watches. A car chase involves the sleuth and the killer, tearing up the city streets. The psycho killer hides in the house waiting for the babysitter. The samurai warrior battles a dozen ninja fighters.

In a drama where the action is more subdued, conflict happens. A doctor operates on a patient who codes on the table. An argument starts between a father and daughter about her drug use. After ten years of marriage, a woman discovers her husband cheating on her. A teacher has sex with a student. Parents pray as their daughter lies dying in a hospital bed.

Even in the simplest of moments, conflict happens. Two brothers argue over the best way to save the family farm. A woman leaves the bar with a man, not knowing he is a serial killer. A husband and wife argue where to vacation. Parents sleep while their teenage son sneaks out the window. Two employees exchange digs and quips.

I read a scene for a mystery writer friend. A psycho killer enters the hotel lobby, checks in with a fake driver's license and stolen credit card. He takes his key and goes to his room. End of the scene.

In a word: boring! In more words, nothing happens, no conflict.

Now I suggested two possibilities.

1. Drop the scene and say at the start of the next scene: "The bad guy checked into the hotel." Let's hope it gets better.

2. Punch it up with struggles. The psycho killer notices a security guard eyeing him. An old girlfriend shows up and may tip off someone about him there. The news on a TV in the lobby shows his picture and tells the police are looking for him. The clerk tells him the credit card was declined. So much can make his life difficult. Yeah, we're not rooting for him but even he doesn't have it roses and daffodils.

The smallest of scenes needs struggles. Conflict occurs. Small disagreements lead to bigger ones. The battles get harder. Conflicts come to everyone. And for the sleuth they only get worse.

Conflict = Struggle

Something happens

Dialog, Who Said What

"Just the facts, ma'am."—Joe Friday

"Just one more thing."—Colombo

"Elementary."—Sherlock Holmes

"Who loves you, baby?"—Kojak

"Book 'em, Danno."—*Steve McGarrett*

"Let's be careful out there."—*Sergeant Phil Esterhaus*

"You've gotta ask yourself a question: do I feel lucky? ... well, do ya, punk?!?"—*Dirty Harry*

Famous detectives have catch-phrases, memorable words that often appear in their speech. We hear the phrase, know who it is. The words bring comfort and make us smile sometimes.

More important is how our sleuths talk. What words they say. The pattern of their speech. The cadence of their language.

- An educated sleuth speaks with big words and long sentences.

- The private eye from the wrong side of the tracks peppers his language with street lingo and snappy dialog.

- A cozy sleuth who is a priest talks about the Bible and religious things.

- Police detectives use words like "perp" and "CI" and "suspect."

- In a 1940s mystery, the PI gabs about "a gat (a gun)" and "fingering someone (identifying)" and "a moll (a gangster's girlfriend)."

- A British constable says, "earwig (eavesdropper)" and "fence (someone dealing in stolen property)" and "knowing one's onions (knowledgeable)."

Speech is not just for the sleuth but other characters too. Their background and history and personalities will decide the way they talk. Emotions come across in language. Speech reveals things.

Aggression
Shyness
Intelligence

Happiness
Depression
Love

Things come across in the way people talk.

When creating dialog, avoid talking heads—the moments when two or more characters talk and nothing happens. Action happens when talk occurs. Conflict underlies speech. No two people see eye-to-eye on things. Even when they sound in agreement, hidden agendas exist.

Avoid tags that are impossible. People cannot smile, sneeze, laugh, choke, snarl and cough words. Stick with the basic stuff like "said" and "asked."

Avoid too many adverbs. Avoid where possible "said softly," "said quickly," "said imploringly," and any other "-ly" words. Instead, describe the action.

"I love you, Mary." He leaned toward her and lowered his voice. "Just don't tell your father."

Notice in this example, I didn't use "said softly." In fact, I didn't use "said" at all. Letting the action tie the words to the speaker.

Avoid stilted dialog. People should sound natural when talking. But don't make it too realistic. Avoid "ums" and "ahs," incomplete thoughts, and disjointed conversation.

Stilted: *Will someone please help my daughter who is stuck in a tree. She is trying but cannot get down.*

Not realistic: *Will someone, ah, please help, um, my daughter. In the tree. She's late for her dance recital. Her father cannot come tonight. Don't worry, darling, someone will help.*

Natural: *Help! Please, help! My daughter's stuck in the tree.*

One trick that can help craft a scene is writing the dialog first as it would appear in a play. Then go back and add in the action and narration.

One final suggestion: test your dialog. Find someone to read it aloud. Better yet, have a few friends speak the roles and see if it sounds natural.

Suspense, Hold Your Breath, Be Afraid

You hold your breath and read, knowing something bad will happen to your favorite character. The next moment is fraught with anticipation and fear. Will it be okay? Will something more terrifying happen? Despite your heart pounding hard, you turn the page.

Suspense is knowing something bad will happen with no way to avoid it. All you can do is hope for the best outcome.

How to create suspense?

Something Bad will Happen

Alert the readers about some impending danger or threat. The characters in the story, who everyone cares about, don't know their fate. Slowly and meticulously take them to that moment. When it happens, only two things can occur. The threat vanishes, and we breathe a sigh of relief. Or the bad thing takes place and the reader cringes.

A killer lurks in the shadows of an alley, a straight razor in his hand. A young woman who just learned she is pregnant walks down the street. The razor's blade catches a glint of light from a street lamp, and he steps deeper into the shadows. She continues to walk toward the alley. His breathing quickens, his grip on the razor tightens. She walks faster, closer to the danger. He grins and growls. The street is empty, and she regrets not taking a taxi home.

What happens next?

Notice how I created a sympathetic character, a soon-to-be mother. In the shadows, the psycho killer lurks. The scene goes back and forth between the threat and her growing fear of the unknown. He jumps out. She screams. Someone hears her and comes running, scaring off the threat. Or the killer grabs her and slits her throat.

Time is the Enemy

Something bad will happen, and time is running out. The hero races the clock to prevent a disaster. But choices aren't clear. Again, take the reader to the edge. Make the moment last.

The timer on the bomb is counting down the seconds. Time left: 2:08. Our hero must decide which wire to cut. The red or blue one? Bombers always use the red wire to trigger the explosive. He moves his cutter to clip it. Time left: 1:27. But this bomber has been unpredictable. He may have wired it in reverse. Cut the blue wire then. He slips the cutter over that wire. Time left: 0:53. This explosive has a yellow wire too. Something he'd not seen before this. Maybe that is the trigger wire. Cut it? Time left: 0:27. Or are they dummy wires and something else will detonate the bomb. Time left: 0:05.

Fortunately, the hero makes the right decision. Something jogs his thoughts and he realizes the correct choice. This makes for a shaky hand and a rapid heartbeat. And who knows perhaps this time he will fail.

The Stakes just got Higher

A major crisis is looming. Something terrible will happen. It may be personal to the sleuth or something affecting everyone. Only the sleuth can fix it.

The private investigator works a murder case in Washington, DC. During his investigation, he uncovers a plot to kill the President. Now, he must act, but nobody will listen. The Secret Service scoffs at his ideas. Yet, he knows he must do something. And the assassination will happen in 24 hours.

Notice, the time factor plays in here.

Complications arise

Things get harder. The sleuth may face insurmountable odds. A lesser person would turn and quit but not our hero. Only this one seems impossible.

Our sleuth in rushing to save a young girl. A psycho has kidnapped her and threatens to kill her in twenty minutes. Then the detective gets a call: her son is missing from his school. The kidnapper calls and tells her to stay away unless she wants her son to die. What does she do?

Key takeaways

1. Something bad will happen. If the victim is unaware of the impending danger, it heightens the suspense. Or when he becomes cognizant, it's too late.

2. Deadlines. Time is the enemy. A ticking timebomb.

3. The problems are big. Overwhelming.

4. The problems are piling up. Step by step more issues arise. Things look insurmountable.

5. Build the suspense. Savor it. Take time to get to the good part.

6. Put a character, someone the reader cares about, in jeopardy.

7. Remove the ability to succeed. Let failures intercede. In the end, the big success comes.

More Advice

Show, don't tell

Telling: *The tall man walked through the doorway.*
Showing: *The man ducked as he passed through the doorway to avoid hitting his head.*

Telling: *The bus stopped at the curb.*
Showing: *The bus driver tooted the horn twice as he pulled up.*

Telling describes an action or happening. Showing demonstrates it.

Use active voice, not passive

Passive: *The rock was thrown by him.*
Active: *He threw the rock.*

Passive*: He was running across the lawn.*
Active: *He ran across the lawn.*

Notice in the passive sentences "was" is used to link the subject with the verb. This holds for "were", "are" and "is." Eliminate those words and make sentences active.

Use strong verbs

He walked down the street.
He strutted down the street. (better)

He pulled the trigger.
He squeezed the trigger. (better)

He made a fist.
He clenched his fist. (better)

Language has so many wonderful words. Use the best word for the moment. Especially consider the verb.

Eliminate excessive "-ly" words

He ran quickly down the street.
He dashed down the street. (better)

Margo talked rapidly about her summer vacation.
Margo babbled on about her summer vacation. (better)

Words ending in -ly are adverbs and used to pump up weak verbs. Best is to eliminate the adverbs and use stronger verbs.

Replace overused words

Examples: saw, heard, thought, little, looked, that, really, then, as, if, and so on.

Often these words are used repeatedly in writing. Most writers have favorites. Used too often, they lose their value.

Use "said" and "asked" rather than fancier words

"I don't love you," he mumbled.
"I don't love you, he said. (better)

"Are you new to town," she inquired.
"Are you new to town?" she asked. (better)

Words that join a quote with the speaker are called "tags." The more unobtrusive they are the better. Sticking with "said" and "asked" keeps them minimally invasive and allows the reader to identify who his speaking. Also, some tags are impossible. People cannot spit, laugh, smile, cry or yawn words.

Avoid clichés

Some clichés are obvious.

Grass is always greener.

Best thing since sliced bread.

The early bird catches the worm.

Slow as molasses in January.

Wet behind the ears.

Others are subtler and can slip into writing.

Against all odds.

Benefit of the doubt

Hand to mouth

In a jam

Moment of truth

Start from scratch

Leave out clichés. Use original ideas, metaphors and similes. The exception may be when quoting someone. Even then avoid the cliché when possible.

Avoid word echoes

Avoid using the same word over and over in a short span of writing. Consider these paragraphs.

Mary saw the time and considered leaving the party early. Then she saw Jim arrive. He saw her and waved across the room. (Too many "saw" words.)

Arriving early is a good thing. Occasionally, it is good to be late. Knowing when to arrive early and when late is good. (Too many "good" words.)

Chapter Three:
Fixing Plot, Character, and Scenes

The Big Picture

You finished your book. If it's your first, the moment can be exhilarating. Months ago, maybe a year or better, you started the journey writing an opening line, introducing the characters, laying out a murder mystery, tossing out clues, perhaps some red herrings, the sleuth revealing the killer, and tidying up loose ends. You finally type those famous two words. THE END.

Whew! Finished, at last.

Sorry but no. Now the fun begins. Many writers dread this part of the process. Some cringe. Others put the story on the shelf and go off on a new project. What is left to do?

Much.

Now the real writing begins.

The first task is to read and reread your mystery novel. The job in the first draft is to get it all down. No attempt is made to write beautiful sentences and stunning paragraphs. In fact, much advice says to avoid rewriting during the first draft. Keep the momentum. Full speed ahead; damn the whatever.

The task at hand is to make it the best ever.

Goal = Make it read like a Mystery

Read, Fix, Repeat

You've rewritten and rewritten.

The story should begin to feel like a mystery novel. Chapters and scenes are defined. You've become proud of it. Now, the real work is about to begin.

Here are things that need checking. Doing some read throughs is best advice. Trying to fix too many things at one time means something will be missed. The task can become overwhelming. It is easy to abandon the project and move on. But now is the time to stay the course.

Below are lists of potential issues. Many repeat across the different character types but they should be checked for each player in your novel. Some seem overly simple. but things happen. I know one writer who changed the name of his sleuth midway through the book and didn't catch it!

The Sleuth

Is the sleuth's name consistent throughout the story?

Is his or her special skill as a sleuth used and put to the test? Does it help solve the crime?

Are his or her flaws presented?

Is he or she compelling?

Is his or her character likable?

Is appearance revealed early?

Are likes and dislikes shown?

Are personality traits demonstrated and consistent?

Is any history of the character included?

Is his speech and way of talking shown and consistent? Does he use a favorite catchphrase or saying?

The Killer

Is his or her name consistent throughout the story?

Is he or she a formidable killer and adversary for the sleuth?

Are backstory details and secrets revealed?

Is appearance shown?

Are likes and dislikes shown?
Are personality traits demonstrated and consistent?
Is any history of the character included?
Is his speech and way of talking shown and consistent?

The Suspects and Victim

Is his or her name consistent throughout the story?
Do they fit their roles?
Are backstory details and secrets revealed?
Is appearance shown?
Are likes and dislikes shown?
Are personality traits demonstrated and consistent?
Is any history of the character included?
Is his speech and way of talking shown and consistent?

The Other Characters

Is his or her name consistent throughout the story?
Do they fit their roles?
Is their appearance described?
Are likes and dislikes shown?
Are personality traits demonstrated and consistent?
Is any history of the character included?
Is speech and way of talking shown and consistent?

Locations

Are locations identified?
Do they hold secrets and backstory?
Does the location present a personality, quirks, and nuances unique to it?
Do the locations have a history?
For geographic locales, do the residents present special speech patterns, slang, idioms, and foreign phrases.

Means, Motive, Opportunity

Do suspects and the killer have means, motive and opportunity?

Does the killer have all three?

Clues and Red Herrings

Are the clues discovered or identified by the sleuth?

Are they found at a location, under particular circumstance?

Do they point to a suspect or the killer?

Are red herrings introduced?

Is there a Key Clue that can only be associated with the killer?

Plot

Does the murder happen soon in the story?

Is the sleuth identified in the first few chapters?

Are the suspects and killer introduced early in the story?

Does the sleuth experience ups and downs in solving the murder?

Are there complications and major twists?

Does the sleuth develop an assumption about who did it?

Does his or her assumption fall apart?

Does the sleuth reach a dead end?

Does he or she have an "aha" moment and realize who the murder is?

Does the story end on a dramatic conclusion?

Does the sleuth reveal the killer?

Are loose ends tidied up?

Some Grammar Advice

My friend is a grammar stickler. She understands the most obscure rules of punctuation and has no qualms telling you if you violate something. You need not be that good, but you want to be good enough.

An editor, publisher, or reviewer needs to see competent writing. This means following the basic grammar rules and spelling words correctly. In a nutshell, your mystery novel must say "professional."

Learn the basics of grammar and punctuation. When not done well, these wave red flags and say amateur. The Internet has lots of information or buy a book. Here are areas to focus on.

- Capitalization

- Punctuation

- Comma usage

- Know the correct homophone—their-there-they're, to-too-two, and so forth

- Correct handling of adverbs and adjectives

- Verb tense.

- Subject-verb agreement

- Unusual punctuations like the semicolon, colons, ellipses and so on.

- Spelling

Spell checkers are great. Just understand the checker cannot interpret what you mean. The word may be spelled properly but not in the current usage.

Grammar checkers are available. **Grammarly** and **ProWritingAid** can review your work but have subscription costs. A search online can find free ones too. Just keep in mind these are tools. Any problems they flag should be reviewed and corrected only if needed. The grammar checker may not understand your intent or meaning.

An error or misspelling doesn't mean the end of the world. Many published books have mistakes if you search for them. Still too many errors in your manuscript and an agent or publisher will stop reading and decide it's not worth their effort.

To be a good writer, learn the basics of grammar and spelling.

Getting Some Criticism

Have someone read your book to find problems and gain insights. As writers, we become too familiar with our own work and miss the proverbial tree. Fresh eyes can be helpful.

Be careful who reads it. Mom, dad, aunt Suzy, a friend, or family member may not help much. Most often they will give you high praise and words of positive worth. Keep in mind: these readers are not experts, and they like you. So, they'll like your book too.

Find independent readers, who need not be nice. Sometimes criticism is hard to take, but getting good advice is priceless. Good critiquers flag what's right and what needs work.

As in other things, online groups exist for getting reviews. They also require giving critiques. Most have rules and guidelines. Follow them.

Here are a few groups I found online.

Critique Circle
https://www.critiquecircle.com/

The Desk Drawer
http://www.winebird.com/

Mystery Writers Forum
http://mwf.ravensbeak.com/forum/index.php

Writing to Publish
http://www.cuebon.com/ewriters/index.html

Locate a face-to-face group locally when possible. Places to look are libraries, bookstores and possibly meetup.com for your location. If you can't locate a group, start one. Ask the library for a meeting space. They'll be happy to let you put up a notice. Allow the group time to grow. Remember, it only takes two to exchange critiques. More people make it better.

Give a critique

Get a critique

Listen to Your Story

Finally, listen to your story. Word and Adobe have built in functions that read the words aloud. Free software for text to speech is available online. Granted the voices are flat and tinny, but hearing your story makes it so much easier to find typos, wording issues, and sentence flow. If you have a friend who can read well that can work too. Just be cautious! The human brain is good at filling in missing words and making corrections on the fly. Someone reading your work may be editing it for you!

The Most Important Tip on Rewriting

Have fun! It's not just the destination. It's the journey.

Ron D. Voigts

Chapter Four:
Self-Publishing

Where to Publish the Ebook

KDP (Kindle Direct Publishing) is the biggest game in ebook town. Amazon holds most of the market share here. So, avoiding them can cut into the profits. Best to go with the winner. For ebooks priced $2.99 and higher, your profit is 70% of the selling price. Sell 100 books at $2.99 each, and that net comes out to be $210. Nice, huh? You can price cheaper, down to 99 cents an ebook but profits drop to 35%. The 100 books now net $35. Still you may sell more books at 1/3 the price. Remember, you are the publisher here; you set the price.

When you publish your ebook with Amazon, you can enroll in KDP Select. It offers good options which I'll cover later in this tome. And I will give you the alternatives to it. For now, enrolling in KDP Select means staying exclusive on Amazon. No publishing anywhere else. The term is for 90 days. More about this later.

Not everyone stays just on Amazon. The next biggie is **Smashwords**. The nice thing about them is they distribute to other sources that KDP does not touch, including Apple, Barnes and Nobles, Overdrive and Kobo. They pay better at lower prices. Ebook sales still net 70% but the bottom drops to 99 cents. Putting a book out for free is okay too. KDP does not offer that choice, at least not directly. More later on that.

Other ebook self-publishers exist. Check your favorite search engine to find them. Many charge a fee. Publish with Amazon and Smashwords for free. You can also go with Kobo and Barnes and Noble. My advice is staying with Amazon and Smashwords as they cover most distribution points.

Paperback Self-Publishing

Writers dream of paperbacks, seeing their name on shiny covers, autographing books at a retail outlet, and showing their friends and relatives a physical book. The truth is most sales are ebooks. Numbers very. In my own books, I mostly sell digital. Paperback works better for well-known writers like Michael Connelly, James Lee Burke, and Lee Child. My experience has been about 100-to-1 for ebooks. In fact, for some of my books, I chose not to go paper, just ebooks.

For a long time, the go-to-place for a paperback was CreateSpace. Most writers went to Amazon for the ebook and CreateSpace for paperback. The two meshed well. Then Amazon bought CreateSpace, and the synergy got better.

Now KDP Paperback is where to go. The method works much like publishing the ebook. Some of the information is already there from setting up the ebook. Complete the paperback details, and Amazon links them together.

Pricing is trickier. The basic formula goes like this.

Fixed cost + (page count x page cost) = printing cost

For a 300-page book with a nice color glossy cover, the printing cost is this.

85 cents + (300 pages x .012 cents/page) = $4.45

This is the cost for you to buy the book outright plus a shipping charge. Buy 20 copies for less than $100 and sell them outright for a tidy profit.

Once set up by KDP, Amazon fills orders one or more at a time, publishing the paperback book soon after the order comes in, which is otherwise known as print-on-down (POD). The books gets wrapped and shipped immediately. Someone with Prime has their book in two days.

Here is an interesting trick. Sometimes Amazon lists alternate sellers. The paperback for ***Great Beginnings (Writing the Killer Mystery)*** has "1 used for $6.40, 5 new for $5.99." These sellers do the same thing; buy POD and drop ship. This is why that one used book says, "Used— Like New" because it is!

Back to the 300-page book. On Amazon it sells for more, but you set any price as long as it stays above a minimum.

Print cost / 60% (royalty rate) = Minimum List Price

$4.45 / 60% = $7.42

The net between the minimum list price and printing cost is Amazon's cut. List the paperback book for $12.99 on Amazon and make $5.57, the difference.

Printing cost + Amazon's cut + Author profit = List price

$4.45 + $2.97 + $5.57 = $12.99

Amazon will distribute your book in other markets but the author's share drops because of added distribution costs. Still it's a win-win. Just keep in mind the ebook sales will eclipse the paperback sales in quantity and dollars in most cases.

Benefits of KDP Select

When publishing with Amazon, many authors opt into KDP Select. It's a 90-day commitment requiring exclusivity on Amazon. Publishing the ebook anywhere else is a no-no. Paperback is okay with other sellers.

Some terms to know.

KENP = Kindle Edition Normalized Pages

KU = Kindle Unlimited

KOLL = Kindle Owners Lending Library

A benefit of KDP Select if you do nothing else is participation in KU and KOLL. With KU, people borrow books, read and return them. If you are in KDP Select then a small box will appear on your book page saying "Kindle, $0.00, Kindle Unlimited" making your book appear free. I often advertise my books "Free with Kindle Unlimited." KOLL covers ebooks lent on Prime.

The Normalized Page is a standard ebook page devised by Amazon and used to determine total page count read for an ebook. If the whole book nets 100 KENPs then someone who reads half the book yields

50 credits. Amazon tracks total KENPs each month. It sets aside a pot of money and divides money based on the author's share for the month. Actual amounts can vary. But let's say one KENP yields 1/2 cent. A credit of 1200 KENPs for an ebook generates $6. This varies but some ebooks do well.

Amazon awards "KDP Select All-Stars" each month for the most-read authors and most-read titles in the U.S., U.K. and Germany. This is a bonus besides regular KENP payments.

If you like being in KDP Select, you can opt in and stay for another 90 days.

Kindle Countdown Deal

A time-based promotional discount of your book, this can be a way to bolster sales. You set the start date and end date for your book's sale. Customers will see the regular price and the special offer. A timer shows how long the deal lasts. The nice thing here is 70% royalty rates are preserved even down to 99 cents. And Amazon has a dedicated website for the specials.

"Free" Book Promotion

Like the Kindle Countdown Deal, you can offer your ebook for free for a limited time. Why do this? Goodwill and visibility help sales. Having many readers increases the likelihood of reviews. Another effect includes getting the first book of a series into the reader's hands, creating interest for subsequent books. After the giveaway ends, residual sales can boom for days, maybe weeks.

Run an Ad Campaign

Sponsored Products. When an Amazon customer enters keywords, they get a list of books matching the search. Near the top of the list, flagged books appear as "sponsored." Opting into this type of ad campaign, your book can appear in the "sponsored" list.

Product Display Ads. Here when a customer goes to a book page, targeted books appear with a group showing "Sponsored Products Related to this Item." As earlier, joining this ad campaign can put your books into the list.

Both are based on clicks, meaning you do not pay unless someone clicks the link. You set the click-price and amounts you wish to spend. Amazon has minimums so check with them.

Beyond KDP Select

If you don't go with KDP Select, you don't get the KENP benefit. No one will borrow your book and you get no payments. Sometimes enrollment pays and other times not. Suggestion here is trying KDP Select for 90 days and see if you do well. I know writers who make a bundle on the KOLL and KU lending. Others don't do well. All I can say is to try it.

KDP Select may not be of much benefit to some writers. But putting your book on Smashwords with listings on Apple and Barnes & Nobel and other places may net more sales than KDP Select. The choice is yours.

You can run sales on your books without KDP Select. Say your book is $2.99, and you run a 99 cents sales. Go to KDP and change the price. It's as simple as that. You can change it on Smashwords but remember it takes time to trickle through the distribution chain. Personally, I only run the sale price on Amazon.

Another cautionary note, Amazon always matches lower prices. If for example you drop Smashwords to 99 cents and keep Amazon at $2.99 and Amazon discovers it, they will drop your book to 99 cents.

This brings up free books. On Smashwords, you can list your book for free. Why do this? It gets the first book in a series into readers' hands. If they enjoy the first story, they may buy the rest of the series. Problem is if it appears on Smashwords or its distribution chain as free, Amazon will drop your book to free status. Once free, it never goes back up on Amazon.

This is Permafree. It may not be a bad thing. Many writers want this so they continue giving away Book 1 and get sales on the rest of the series. The philosophy is go Permafree on Amazon and keep Smashwords free too.

Coupons at Smashwords

Smashwords allows coupons for sales and specials. Following are the parameters.

Coupon discount—1 to 66% or 100% off

Promotional discount—$0.99 to $2.98, or 0.00

Adjust either one and the Smashwords Coupon Manager will give you the net proceeds from a sale.

End date can be set no farther out than 5 years.

Meter redemption fixes the maximum number of uses. Use for a special like "good for only the first 10 buyers."

Making a coupon public is possible. Then it will show up on the Smashwords sale page.

Smashwords will generate a special code number for your sale.

Here is how it looks for my book *Claws of the Griffin*.

Promotional price: $0.99
Coupon Code: YJ23E
Expires: November 12, 2018
Description:
Redemptions (max): N/A
Public: Yes

The Smashwords sales page for this book if it is made public looks like this.

*Use the code **YJ23E** at checkout for 67% off*

(Offer good through Nov. 12, 2018)

Where to go next?

Self-publishing has hurdles. At a minimum, you must do the following.

- Edit the book for publication

- Design a book cover

- Format the book for Kindle

- Format the book for POD

Some other things may come up as well on the promotion side.

- Design a website

- Email promotion

I have always been a DIY person and self-taught on most of these matters. For some it may be a daunting task. Others may see it as an exciting moment to grow in the craft.

If doing stuff on your own is not your thing, then find someone who can help. Prices can vary and costs roll up. Following are possible fees. As seen, this can be expensive and cost a few hundred dollars.

- Design a book cover, $25 to $300

- Format the book for Kindle/POD, $25 to $250

- Edit the book for publication, $50 to $600

- Design a website, $50 to $300

A good place to shop is *Fiverr.com* where you can find people and prices that work for you.

If you are a do-it-yourself type, check out some books on Kindle or search online. I learned much of what I needed to know by brute force and plodding ahead.

Someone showing how it's done is another great way to learn. *Udemy.com* has courses on just about anything. Author, mentor, and teacher Brian Jackson offers several courses for self-publishing and marketing, and I recommend them. He walks you through what you need to know with lots of visual and detailed explanations. Check out these courses at the following location.

https://www.udemy.com/user/brianjackson13/

- Beginner Wordpress Website Design and Wordpress Development
- Amazon eBook Self-publishing/Self-publish Publishing/Publish
- Amazon Self-publishing: Self-publish a Kindle/Paperback Book
- Book Covers for Self-publishing: Self-publish w/PowerPoint
- GIMP 2.8/GIMP 2.10: Beginners: Free GIMP Book Covers
- MailChimp Mailing List Building & MailChimp Email Marketing

For readers of *Writing the Killer Mystery*, use coupon code WEBDEAL10 to get them for $10 each.

Chapter Five:
Traditional Publishing

Publishers and Literary Agents and Writers, Oh my!

A long time ago, booksellers operated from physical buildings on streets. The books they sold came in two varieties, hardcovers and paperbacks, both with real paper. Independent proprietors stocked books on shelves from floor to ceiling. The hottest new reads appeared in displays near the front door and in the windows.

Big-name publishers controlled what went into the displays. The bestselling authors received upfront promotion space. Their names became household words. Their books made the best-seller lists.

Small-house publishers got shelf space too. At times, one of their writers produced a breakout novel and joined the ranks of bestselling authors.

This was the state of the business. Wannabe authors hoped to beat the odds and land book contracts with the big-name and small-house publishers. An intermediary became necessary, someone called the literary agent. The publishers added barriers, wanting only the best manuscripts. Literary agents filled the need, screening books, looking for the next winner. For the writer, the lit agent was the first step on a long road to publication.

Then came the chain bookstores. The mega suppliers had whatever a bibliophile wanted. Shelves no longer stretched to the ceiling but became displays where book seekers shopped and met fellow readers searching for something to read. Easy chairs and reading tables accommodated potential buyers. Games, puzzles, and trinkets added to their product line. A few had coffee shops. Music CDs and video with the latest movies became part of the offering. Most notable was Barnes & Noble.

The chain bookseller brought one more thing. Publishers lacked the clout they once had. The big-name stores decided how their shops appeared and what they sold. Still only two types of publishers existed. Those with big names and deep pockets, and small houses grappling to put out good books. And the literary agents continued to do their job.

The Internet took off, and another publisher joined the fray. This newcomer had a different business model. They'd sell books for electronic readers. Overhead was low (no paper needed), delivery was almost instantaneous, and people carried an entire library around on an electronic device smaller than the average hardcover book. The new company called Amazon named its reading machine the Kindle.

Amazon did one more thing that revolutionized the business. They opened the door for any author looking to publish a book and sell it. The move was brilliant. They created the most revolutionary method to deliver books and leveled the playing field for authors everywhere to become published.

To make things even more interesting, printing books in lots of 5,000 at a time moved on to print-on-demand (POD). Companies such as CreateSpace and Lulu took files from anyone and turned them into paperback books the same day of the order. The publishing world got easier; the mystique and hassle of selling a book vanished.

Two new publisher types came onto the scene. Virtual houses popped up everywhere. The companies operated from home offices, many with publishers, editors, and cover designers linked across the country by email and the Internet. Literary agents still submitted books but this new breed of publisher considered manuscripts directly from authors.

The other newcomer was the self-publisher, an author who removed the middleman from the equation and did it himself, producing books by POD, Kindle, and other ebook formats.

The big-name and small-house publishers took on all the tasks of supporting their authors including marketing. For the virtual publishers, editing, cover design, and formatting became their forte with marketing left up to the author. In the self-publishing realm, everything becomes the author's task.

The virtual publisher's philosophy was "throw it against the wall and see what sticks." Their investment was getting the book out there using low overhead, part-time employees, and volunteer help. For the virtual publishers, the work was a labor of love.

The big names and small houses loved what they do too. But they knew what sticks when it hits the wall and how to make it stay there. The big names had deep pockets and enough clout to take their authors to the top of the best seller list.

The self-publisher could only hope it sticks. They don't have the monetary resources, but many are savvy in marketing and publishing. Some have gone far and done well on their own.

Tier One Publisher

Big-name publishers. Georg von Holtzbrinck Publishing Group/Macmillan, Hachette (publisher), HarperCollins, Penguin Books, Random House, Simon & Schuster

Tier Two Publisher

Small-house publishers. Baen Books, Harlequin Romance, TCK Publishing, Saint Martins Press

Tier Three Publisher

Virtual, indie-publishers

Tier Four Publisher

Self-publishers

Do you need an agent?

Most high-end publishers look to agents for material. The agent does their job, weeding out the not-so-good writers, finding good material. Some agents have a reputation, and their clients are shoo-ins.

Rejection by an agent does not mean you're no good. They reject material for lots of reasons. Does not meet their needs. Too busy to take on another project. Voice of the work doesn't grab them. No tingle when reading it. Often, they will send a brief critique with the rejection. Listen to what they say. Do not take it personally.

Finding an agent can be easy or hard. Timing means everything. Perseverance does not hurt. Most important, read their guidelines for submission and follow it. A little creativity is okay but step outside their rules and they'll not consider it. These are busy people, used to doing things on their terms.

Where to find one?

Check out the Writer's Digest Shop *Guide to Literary Agents 2019* or whatever is the current year.

Search the Internet for "list of literary agents."

Ask another writer about their agent.

Make sure your book is polished, professional, and finished. Non-fiction can be sold on speculation but not fiction. So much is out there for them, they'll pass if you're not ready.

Landing an agent requires a query letter. In the past, the post office delivered your mail to them. You included a return-stamped envelope for their reply. This was a courtesy. My experience was interested agents covered the return postage on communications with you. Rejections came back on your dime. Now, email is the norm. Instead of paper, everything goes over the Internet.

Have a synopsis ready. This can be short or long. Cover the plot basics and major characters. Subplots need not be done. Include the mystery's ending, up to who did it and how the sleuth knew. I prepared two versions, a one page and a longer one, about four pages. The single page version was single spaced with the title and author name at the top. The longer version was double spaced with headers, page numbers, authors name and address, and word count.

Often, an agent asks for sample chapters. Again, have a version of that ready beside the full manuscript. Remember, these are guidelines. Pay attention to what the agent requests and follow it to the letter.

A literary agent should not ask for money. No reading fees. No book doctor fees. The only justifiable costs are postage for sending out your manuscript and copying costs. Most times, I made my own copies and shipped them to the agent. With everything by emails and attachments these days, these expenses should not exist.

Your agent will negotiate all deals on your behalf. The agent's fee is typically 15% of the royalties. You will sign a contract with the agent. If she places your work, then you'll make another contract with the publisher. The publisher pays your agent on your behalf, and she sends you your 85%.

Agents should keep you abreast of the publishers they queried and the responses. My agent blind copied (bcc) me on emails and forwarded the publishers' responses. If you have not heard from your agent for six weeks or so follow up with her. But don't bug her needlessly; they are your agent, not your friend.

Publisher's replies can vary. Most are slow to respond. Again, it will be your agent's responsibility to follow up. You don't contact or deal with the publisher until a contract is signed.

What do Publishers do?

A publisher buys the rights to your book. You sign a contract. They schedule the publish date six months out. All is good.

An editor from the publisher works with you to whip the book into shape. And you thought it was already good. She marks up a copy of your book, usually digitally in a .doc or .docx format. You'll rewrite and send it back. The process repeats. Edit. Rewrite. Repeat.

While the dance of rewriting takes place, they'll ask you to work on the other stuff needed to publish.

- A book blurb, the description appearing on Amazon or the book jacket.

- A logline, a catchy phrase to entice a reader to buy your book.

- You provide book cover ideas, but a final decision is theirs.

- Keywords for Amazon searches.

They'll ask for your marketing ideas. Social media such as Twitter and Facebook will come up. You'll tell them of blogs that'll review your book, and they may have a few their own. Your own website or blog will be pitched as a great launch site. If not formally, you'll provide an ad hoc plan to get the word out.

Now if you are lucky or talented and get a big-name publisher, they'll do much of this stuff but don't get too happy. You'll still tour and make appearances, go to book signings and speaking engagements.

A book series is a good thing. The publisher may make a contract to do all your books. You just send more their way. The process outlined above repeats.

The good thing about a publisher is their support with book covers, edits, final polish and editing. You'll help with marketing. You'll feel you're not alone. The publisher takes a cut of your book sales, and a literary agent may get her share too. They limit your control, setting prices, offering giveaway books, and marketing, things you control when self-publishing.

The final choice is yours.

Chapter Six:
Marketing, You got to have a plan

Making Friends, Finding Fans

I posed a question years ago when I published my first book. The meaning behind it will soon become clear and offer insight to selling books. Here is that profound question.

After selling your book to friends and family, who else will buy it?

For a new writer, here's what happens.

Your first book comes out. Whether you self-published or went traditional, your labor of love is out there for the world to buy. Dreams of big sales and more books fill your head like others think about winning the lottery. Money is not even the object, only book sales.

Things start well. Sales come in as friends and family buy your book. Even a few stray sales occur. Months later demand for the book tapers. More time passes, and the flow falls to almost nil if not totally dry.

Subtracting friends and family from the equation shows sales were not as good as they seemed. Yes, people buy new books. But the moment fades.

Writers with great networks sell many books initially. Others with fewer contacts sell fewer books. But eventually sales converge to nothing.

Here's another story. I know a writer who wrote his first book. As books go, it was okay. Lots of action. Not a masterpiece by any means. He developed a large network of acquaintances, friends, bloggers, people he met along the way. His book took off. Those people wrote reviews, lots of them. Sales stayed brisk, and the reviews topped over 100 in the first month. Momentum carried things forward. Years later, his book continues to sell with little effort. The monthly quantity is not near what it had been, down in the 20-30 range. Still not bad considering he published the book five years ago, and he's not produced another since.

41

So, what's his secret? He'd found enough followers to create the momentum. Some writers call it critical mass. He had sufficient people to buy his book and got the boulder rolling downhill. Even without further support his book continues to sell. Five years so far have been a good run.

Most writers call their followers fans, but "friends" is a better term. These are people who feel close to the author even if they have never met outside the realm of literature. They show up at book signings, visit Facebook pages with kudos, and line up to buy the next book. Writers who have these many fans have reached critical mass.

What is the magic number? I don't know if an exact value exists that guarantees success, and it may vary from author to author. The number often thrown out is 1,000 fans. Maybe it's only 500. Perhaps it's 1,500. But let's use 1,000 for now.

So, if you want to become a successful writer, finding 1,000 fans (AKA friends) can be daunting. Downright scary in fact. But there is good news.

You make friends, one at a time.

Know Your Audience

Writers write books, often without considering who reads them. Knowing your readers is important. Their demographics determine what books to write and the marketing strategy.

Murder Mystery Readers

- 25% of readers are over the age of 65

- Over 50% are between 30 and 64 years-old

- Women outnumber men by better than 2-to-1

Takeaway: the largest audience will be middle-age women, followed by seniors. The smallest group are teens and twenty-somethings.

So why this focus? Readers identify with the protagonist. You will want the detective to be someone who they see as themselves. The most popular sleuth is a woman in her forties and fifties. The next biggie is the senior woman solving crimes. This does not mean neglecting other groups so read on.

Most cozy mysteries have a middle-age, female sleuth; a senior works well too. Remember this sub-genre downplays sex, language, and violence and the murder happens most often offstage. Humor is important for this group of readers.

A note: women have fewer issues reading mysteries with a male sleuth, but men are less likely to identify with a female. So, a middle-aged or senior male sleuth can also work for either gender in a cozy.

What mysteries do men read? Police procedural and private eye are at the top. The tough, macho, glib talking male sleuth is often the choice. Men may gravitate toward a female sleuth if she is sexy, able to handle herself, and resourceful.

Readers cross boundaries but most stay in their demographic. I don't want to sound biased or sexist, but people read what they read, and it does not hurt to be cognizant of what will sell.

Branching out in the other sub-genres poses challenges. Many of the choices show the nuances of the crossover genres.

If an SF mystery is your thing, then consider getting up to speed in the realm of speculative fiction. Most readers will be guys with the men outnumbering women by 3-to-1 (although the gap is closing). The sleuth will be a male. Another thing, these readers are educated and savvy so know your stuff here.

Romance mysteries are popular and dominate much of the romance business. The readership of women to men is 4-to-1 and fall into the 25 to 39 age group. Here, sticking to a formula for romance writing is imperative. The sleuth is usually a woman and the POV character. Her romantic target is always a handsome male. They are compatible but aren't clicking. In the meantime, she is solving a murder.

Writing the Killer Mystery: Great Beginnings identifies over forty sub-genres. The number is too vast to cover in this section. Rather, the best way to focus on your particular sub-genre is to read books in the area and get a feel for the writing. Keep in mind the demographics of your reader when creating the sleuth and storyline.

Understanding your reader is the first step in marketing since that is who you sell to. You will need to find who most likely will buy your book. Focus on writing and selling to that group.

Making Friends on Social Media

Facebook

https://www.facebook.com

One of the biggie social media sites is Facebook. FB is not itself a book selling site but a place to meet people and make friends. If you've not tried FB, give it a shot and sign up.

Facebook by itself is not a place to build an author following but rather make friends. This social site is where your say what's on your mind. Some people post their day-to-day activities, others use it to catch up with folks, and many share interesting stuff. Whatever, have fun.

After your personal page, you want a "Community or Public Figure" page with your page name and category. Mine is "Author Ron D. Voigts" and "Author". Then upload a profile picture and banner photo at the top. You can post about your writing. Unlike your personal FB page where you "make friends", you'll collect "likes" on your author page. Many writers use their FB author page like a website or blog for posting about their writing and books.

Twitter

https://twitter.com

Twitter is less about friends and more about acquaintances. You want to set up an account. Add a profile picture and banner and mini bio. These images should target your writing. As you add "Followers," you want to target categories like mystery, writer, reader and stretch beyond the obvious. I always check horror, thriller, and crime.

Posts, AKA tweets, can be up to 280 characters long. Hashtags are popular. I use #amreading, #amwriting, and #Kindle in my tweets. Tweets from users stream continuously. Just jump in and ride along. A good practice is tweeting about other authors and their books. You can also retweet something you like.

Goodreads

https://www.goodreads.com

A website for readers and book recommendations. Start an account and make friends. You can catalog your books, share what you're reading and post reviews on the ones you've finished. Communities, groups and discussions await on every genre and interest and aspect of books.

Create an author page and update its profile. Link it to your blog. Gain followers. Manage your friends. When you join groups, stay with the groups' focus. Don't push your own books on them. Let them accept you.

Other social media tools.

Pinterest (**https://www.pinterest.com/**) — image sharing.

Tumblr (**https://www.tumblr.com**) — allows blogging and sharing.

Instagram (**https://www.instagram.com**) — photo sharing app.

Youtube (**https://www.youtube.com**) — post video content about your books.

Google+ (**https://plus.google.com**) — find communities with similar interest.

LinkedIn (**https://www.linkedin.com**) — professional networking, finding other writers.

Medium (**https://medium.com**) — blogging platform. Use as standalone or in parallel with another blog.

Library Thing (**https://www.librarything.com**) — similar to Goodreads.

Social Media Do's and Don'ts

1. Get involved with the community. Don't push sales of your books.

2. Don't make it all about you. Share in their worlds.

3. Set aside time to update your social media. Make it a regular event.

4. Stay for the long haul. Build your presence slowly.

5. Respect your friends and readers. These are your audience.

6. Promote other authors and their books.

7. Don't let social media consume you. There is a life beyond it.

8. Make friends.

9. Remember to write.

10. Have fun.

Reviews, What Others Think

Reviews are the dirty little secret from Amazon. You need them. How many is a good question. A successful writer friend told me once that a book needed at least 35 reviews. Other sources say a minimum of 7 reviews is needed. Best answer, you need reviews. No reviews = not good.

The secret part is getting the reviews. Most people don't write reviews. They buy your book. They love it. Then they go onto the next one. Though opinions vary, only one-in-a-hundred sales will turn into a review. Some say the odds are even higher. Getting reviews this way is slow going.

Amazon has cracked down on the terms of reviews. Among the highlights, they cannot be purchased or gained by other compensation such as gifts or prizes. Members of the same household or close friends cannot review your book. Amazon can take down a review, no questions asked. Here is a great link for FAQ.

https://www.amazon.com/gp/community-help/customer-review-guidelines-faqs-from-authors

So, what can you do?

1. Their friends and family clause can be sketchy. Don't have family members with the same last name review. Most friends and associates are okay, so ask people at work and at school and at church.

2. At the end of your book, after THE END, add something like this.

If you enjoyed this book, I'd be grateful if you posted a short review on Amazon. Your opinion is important and I read all reviews. Thank you.

Then supply a weblink to reviews for your book. Since they can be long, use bit.ly or your favorite URL shortening service. Put the link after the review request. Check at the end of this book for an example of how mine looks.

If you self-publish, be sure to ask for a review. If you go with a traditional publisher, ask them to add it.

3. Contact other authors and ask them to buy and review your book. You can return the favor for their books. Facebook is a good place to find other authors looking for reviews. Check on groups that exchange reviews. Here are a few. Enter the name in the FB search engine and click <Join>.

Kindle Review Swap and Author Advice

Kindle Book Review Exchange

Kindle Books Promotion & Review Swap

When swapping with someone you don't know, here is some advice. If you found them on FB, you will want to use private messaging (PM) to contact them. Insist they send you a screenshot of the purchase and you do the same. Agree to post reviews no later than two weeks. Finally ask for a screen shot of the review. Both can be exchanged by FB PM.

Don't get stiffed. You have 7 days to return an ebook on Amazon. I recommend not even starting to read their book until you have a confirmation they purchased yours. If it goes without proof they bought your book, then return theirs.

If you post your review and don't get one in return, contact the author by FB PM. Remember you have 60 days to delete your review. Don't be shy. I have deleted a few reviews. Don't accept a sob story. You both had an agreement. The mutual review exchange was what was agreed. My own experience has been that one in five review swaps fall apart. Worse case you are out the cost of an ebook. Hence, I stick to 99 cent ebooks where possible.

4. Give away books. Amazon permits reviews of books not purchased but gifted for reviews. The major difference is a purchased book will have "verified purchase" flagged with the review. The giveaway will not.

The other rule to follow is anyone reviewing a book that was gifted to them should identify it in the review. "I received this book in exchange for an honest review." Of course, this may be hard to enforce.

Where to find reviewers —
Goodreads
Library Thing
Facebook Groups
Bloggers

Gifting a book to a blogger will get a mention and possibly a review on their website. They may even drop one on Amazon. Other potential reviewers can be hit and miss when given a free book. It's a calculated risk.

Best if you can offer a .mobi. A PDF works but risks releasing a more copyable ebook. If you published on Smashwords, you can offer them coupons for free books.

Getting the Word Out with Mail Lists

Many writers have great success with mail lists. Basically, you manage a list of subscribers who have agreed to receiving emails. You cannot just add names and email addresses to a list but rather need people who sign up. Signing up people without their permission violates US and International spam laws.

You can keep your own list and send emails from your own email account, but this can become tedious. Some email providers have limits on how many emails you can send out, again to prevent spamming.

An alternative to doing it yourself is a service such as MailChimp.com who provides the tools to manage the lists. The process goes like this.

1. MailChimp will assist and support a customizable, sign-up page with a URL to collect email addresses, names, and other info. They can provide an HTML version to integrate into your website or blog. You advertise your mail list as a newsletter or something as that. Offering a free-gift for signing up such as a download of an ebook helps find new followers.

2. Next if you check the option, another page pops up with a CAPTCHA notice. That is one of those opt-in devices to prevent spambots from automatically signing up to your newsletter. It asks them to verify a human signing up to your email list.

3. Another option is a response email sent to the potential follower asking them to confirm their desire to join the email list. They click a link and poof they're in.

4. The final option is a Welcome email telling how happy you are they joined. This is where I put information regarding the free download I promised.

At a minimum, you must do step 1 above. Steps 2 through 4 are optional but recommended. They help insure your new followers are humans and not someone using another's email.

If you wish to see this process in action, go to the beginning or end of this volume and sign up to my newsletter. You will see how these four steps work.

MailChimp allows you to mass email to your followers. You can even personalize them with their names embedded. Most writers stick to a schedule. The key here is not to overwhelm someone. Too many emails too often turns off readers who may unsubscribe.

Mail templates allow you to send out a professional appearing newsletter. These have pictures, headlines, words, links, columns and more. Make it what you want, simple or complex. Just remember, the more professional you are, the more apt they are to read the content.

What do you write about? Remember the 80-20 rule. Most of the content is stuff interesting to the readers. Since you are writing Mysteries, keep the focus around that. Discuss the craft, review books, do author interviews, tell of new mystery movies. This is akin to writing a blog. Look for themes. Around Halloween talk about haunted houses and spooky stuff. Christmas time, showcase mysteries about the season and maybe a mystery cookie recipe. Be creative!

The other 20% is what you're doing. Talk about your books, tell about specials and discounts, what you are writing. If you do book signings or appear at cons, then give out your schedule. Alert them to any new ebooks coming up. You might be able to find beta readers here for your next book and get a review or two.

MailChimp allows analytics. You can track your newsletter readers, their clicks on links and so forth. This helps determine your best followers and who might be receptive to something new. You can segment the list and pick who gets a particular newsletter.

MailChimp is free for the first 2,000 followers. Paid subscriptions start at $10 a month. A premium version exists but is much pricier.

If MailChimp is not your bag of bananas, alternatives exist. I don't know them well or their pricing but here they are.

Get Response (**https://www.getresponse.com**)

Sparkpost (**https://www.sparkpost.com**)

Active Campaign (**https://www.activecampaign.com**)

Maropost (**https://www.maropost.com**)

AWeber (**https://www.aweber.com/home.htm**)

Websites and Blogs and Other Sundry Things

Some writers have websites and others don't. Some insist they are absolute necessities, and others could not care less. Whatever route you go, you must decide what's in it for you.

Start a Blog

A blog is an easy way to get word out about your writing. Many writers go to **http:\\blogger.com**. You can sign up for an account and design your blog site. The main goal here is blogging but you can go with sidebar entries such as pics of your books and links to their listings on Amazon or wherever you sell them. Blogging requires dedication. A post a week works well. People come back and check out what is happening. Here are ideas to blog about.

Stuff about your books

Reviews of books in the mystery genre

Authors in the mystery genre

Discussion of writing mysteries

Things related to mysteries

You can nearly blog on anything; just ask yourself how it relates to your writing. This is not the time to discuss your political or religious beliefs. The point is to make friends. Your job is to sell books.

Get a Website

A website makes you look professional. You will need a host for it. Bluehost.com, hostgator.com and godaddy.com are a few places to host your site.

Next, you need a website. Someone can do it for you. Costs differ upward to a few hundred dollars. Fivver.com has people to help for a fee. You can head out on your own too. Most do-it-yourselfers use Wordpress with some canned package. A DIY website is not a cakewalk but can be done.

Your website will have a static page where you introduce yourself, talk about your latest book, and provide links to deals and places to buy your books. Another page can showcase your books with links. Other pages include "About Me", "Contact Info", and even stuff like Galleries (pictures) and email opt-ins. Everything ends up with a nice menu bar putting stuff a click away. You can add a blog for letting your readers know what's on your mind. Remember, as you gain popularity, people will want to keep up with what you're doing, what's coming up next, and just your thoughts.

Find Bloggers

Like you, other writers and readers are interested in mysteries. Search for their websites. Find their contact information. Many specialize in reviewing books. Just remember these are busy people. Email them. Offer a review copy of your book. Suggest an author interview or a guest blog by you. The point here is you want to make friends with them and their readers.

Seven Keywords for SEO

When setting up your mystery novel on KDP, you need seven keywords for Search Engine Optimization. Not clear but you can use phrases for each keyword; using a single word can hurt getting your book noticed when someone searches on Amazon. The right phrases give the best chances for someone to find your book. Here is a simple formula to find the best keywords.

Determine Usable Phrases

1. Find single words that pertain to your mystery novel. The obvious ones are MYSTERY, DETECTIVE, CRIME, and MURDER.

2. Take a hard look at your book. Think about the subgenre. For a medical mystery, you might try DOCTOR, HOSPITAL, NURSE, MEDICINE, and HEALTH.

3. You can check AMAZON books like your own. I found these for medical mysteries. GHOST, SURGERY, MEDICAL CENTER, and BLOOD.

4. The next step is to find actual phrases. Use an Incognito window like in Google Chrome. This reduces chances that an earlier search biases the Amazon search engine.

5. Do the searches on Amazon in the KINDLE STORE.

6. In the search box, enter a target word as found above, then a space and the first letter in the alphabet. The Amazon search function will complete your typing and finish the phrases. Follow through with each alphabet letter.

Entering M-Y-S-T-E-R-Y-space-A, yields the following.

mystery and suspense best sellers

mystery anthologies

mystery and romance

For M-Y-S-T-E-R-Y-space-B, I get these.

Mystery books

Mystery British

Mystery best sellers

For the next letter, I get more.

Mystery cats

Mystery Christian

Mystery castle

Mystery chest

Continue through the alphabet. After hitting Z, go on to the next target word and run the alphabet again. As you move along copy or note the phrases that best suit your mystery.

This method will yield keywords (phrases). Re-enter them. Check out how many hits come up. *Mystery Cats* comes up with 8,000. *Mystery chest* only has 105 books in the search. So, using *Mystery Chest* (if that is your keyword) may be a good choice as your book appears sooner and not get lost in the crowd.

The question is how many people check your keyword. *Mystery chest* may then not be a good choice if few people use that search phrase. These are the hard decisions.

Programs such as KDP Rocket, KD Spy and Kindle Sumarai search for you with information to make a better decision. They also cost a few bucks. So, the choice is yours. Roll up your sleeves and do the work or buy a program to do it for you.

My choice is KDP Rocket. With its help I came up with seven keywords for **Volume 1, Writing the Killer Mystery: Great Beginnings**. Here are the phrases I used and the book's position in the Amazon search at the time of writing this volume.

writing a mystery novel—3
mystery writers handbook–7
how to write a damn good mystery–15
writing and selling your mystery novel–13
how to write a cozy mystery–17
writing a murder mystery–16
how to write mystery novel–13

Give Away Books, Be Generous

Authors give away books. People love freebies. Be judicious with your generosity. Your goal is to sell books but some giveaways are needed.

Who Gets the Giveaways?

1. Reviewers do. You want as many verified reviews on Amazon but often giving away a few is inevitable.

2. Bloggers may want a copy to discuss on their blog.

3. Run a contest, and the winner gets a free copy of your book.

Where to do giveaways

1. Join groups on Goodreads and Library Thing. Finding reviewers is the goal of some groups. Put out a notice. "Ten copies of my book available to anyone who will post a review."

2. Again, bloggers willing to read and give you publicity.

3. Contests. I've done these from Facebook parties. The first person to answer a question correctly gets the freebie.

4. On blogs, I run a Raffle Copter (**https://www.rafflecopter.com/**) giveaway.

How to Giveaway a Book

1. Send a .mobi file to the winner. During the setup on Kindle, you can download a copy. Be sure to get it.

2. If you published on Smashwords, issue a coupon for a free book or two. Remember, you can limit the number. Hold the count to the number of winners.

3. If you did a paperback, you can give away copies. Your price as the publisher will be much lower than the list price. Be

sure to ship by 4th class, book rate with the USPS. Don't forget to autograph.

4. I don't recommend gifting a copy on Amazon. Recipients can cash in the gift and use it for something else.

Giveaways build goodwill. Don't overdo it. Your priority is selling books.

Building Your Author Platform

Marketing books have been the focus, but the reality is you're selling yourself. This is building an author platform, creating a recognizable name that sells books.

Stephen King is a prime example. His name becomes the focal point in book sales. Notice on book covers, his name is at the top in the largest font. The title falls below somewhere. Why? Because people buy his name and not the book's.

This is the recognition having a good author platform achieves.

How do you achieve an author platform?

1. Focus on your writing niche. *Writing the Killer Mystery* is about writing mysteries in general but you need to find your specific area. Look again at the sub-genres presented in Volume One in this series. Readers need to know what you write. Are they medical mysteries? Paranormal? Senior? Or one of the other possibilities. Perhaps you will define a new sub-genre in the mystery realm.

2. Be known for a series. When the series name comes up, fans know you're its writer. Remember the classic writers I mentioned in Volume One? Perry Mason and its author, Erle Stanley Gardner, comes to mind. Sherlock Holmes elicits Sir Arthur Conan Doyle. Another is Ed McBain and The 87th Precinct series. Some current writers doing series are James Lee Burke, Michael Connelly, and Kerry Greenwood, to name a few.

3. On social media, have your name in the forefront. Do a Facebook Author Page. Get your Twitter account started in your name. For the other social media, keep your name out there.

4. For your blog or website, have your name as part of the URL. My site is **http://www.authorrondvoigts.com/**. Avoid using your series or book's name. This has to be about you.

5. Get yourself as much exposure as possible. There never can be too much. Get on blogs, do interviews, hit the social media, and find wherever else you can get your name out. It's about you, the author.

6. Continue to write quality books. You want people to talk about them. You want anticipation about your next one.

7. Publish on a regular basis. Many writers shoot for a book a year. Publish the next volume in a series.

8. Get an email list and stay in touch. Send out newsletters on a regular schedule. Once a month is a nice pace, but you decide what is best. Just don't be a pest.

9. Remember you are a brand just like Coca-Cola, Ford Motor Company, and Burger King. Get exposure. Promote yourself wherever and whenever you can. People must hear your name and think of the books you write.

10. Back to the first thing I said. Make friends. Find fans. It's you who you're selling not just the books.

Chapter Seven:
Last Thoughts

Just a Few Words, Please

Thank you for taking the time to read *Writing the Killer Mystery: Getting It Right, Getting Paid, Volume Five.* The advice in this tome should assist you to get published and recognized as a mystery author. If I've helped and you found this useful, please let others know and write a short review of this book. You can find a link on the Amazon page where your first purchased this book.

Thanks!

Writing the Killer Mystery Series

Volume 1: Great Beginnings (Released April 2018)

- Mystery Writers and Their Sleuths
- Understanding the Mystery
- Types of Mystery
- Got a good idea?

Volume 2: Captivating Characters (Released May 2018)

- The Sleuth
- The Victim
- The Killer
- The Suspects
- Special Characters
- The Rest of the Characters

Volume 3: Plotting the Murder (Released July 2018)

- The Plot
- The Opening
- The Middle Game
- The End
- Scenes

Volume 4: Places, Clues, and Guilt (October 2018)

- Setting
- Means, Motive, Opportunity
- Clues, Red Herrings, Misdirection
- History, Backstory

Volume 5: Getting It Right, Getting Paid (January 2019)

- Writing Advice
- Revision
- Publishing
- Promotion

Note: release dates and content of future volumes are subject to change. Please stop my website at **http://www.authorrondvoigts.com** for updates.

About Ron D. Voigts

Ron writes murder mysteries. His sleuths have included a thirteen-year-old, a psychic, a news reporter, a playboy, a Goth witch, and a suicidal man. Researching a mystery writing class for a college extension course, he undertook to put his experience, knowledge, and skills into a five-volume series laying out easy to understand and apply methods of writing a mystery. Beyond his fiction and non-fiction writing, he creates book covers and edits work for others. Catch more about him at **http://www.authorrondvoigts.com**.

Made in the USA
Monee, IL
06 April 2020